A Note to Parents

DK READERS is a compelling program for beginning readers, designed in conjunction with leading literacy experts, including Dr. Linda Gambrell, Distinguished Professor of Education at Clemson University. Dr. Gambrell has served as President of the National Reading Conference, the College Reading Association, and the International Reading Association.

Beautiful illustrations and superb full-color photographs combine with engaging, easy-to-read stories to offer a fresh approach to each subject in the series. Each DK READER is guaranteed to capture a child's interest while developing his or her reading skills, general knowledge, and love of reading.

The five levels of DK READERS are aimed at different reading abilities, enabling you to choose the books that are exactly right for your child:

Pre-level 1: Learning to read
Level 1: Beginning to read
Level 2: Beginning
        to read alone
Level 3: Reading alone
Level 4: Proficient readers

The "normal" age at which a child begins to read can be anywhere from three to eight years old. Adult participation through the lower levels is very helpful for providing encouragement, discussing storylines, and sounding out unfamiliar words.

No matter which level you select, you can be sure that you are helping your child learn to read, then read to learn!

LONDON, NEW YORK, MUNICH,
MELBOURNE, and DELHI

Senior Editor Helen Murray
Editorial Assistant Ruth Amos
Senior Designer Guy Harvey
Designer Jon Hall
Pre-production Producer Siu Yin Chan
Producer David Appleyard
Managing Editor Elizabeth Dowsett
Design Manager Ron Stobbart
Art Director Lisa Lanzarini
Publishing Manager Julie Ferris
Publishing Director Simon Beecroft

Reading Consultant Linda B. Gambrell

Rovio
Approvals Editor Rollo de Walden
Senior Graphic Designer Jan Schulte-Tigges
Publishing Director Laura Nevanlinna

Hasbro
Director of Global Publishing Michael Kelly
Senior Designer Steven Lathrop
Product Development Specialist Heather Hopkins

First published in the United States in 2014
by DK Publishing
345 Hudson Street, New York, New York 10014

10 9 8 7 6 5 4 3 2 1
001–275289–Nov/14

DK books are available at special discounts when
purchased in bulk for sales promotions, premiums,
fund-raising, or educational use.
For details, contact:
DK Publishing Special Markets
345 Hudson Street
New York, New York 10014
SpecialSales@dk.com

A catalog record for this book
is available from the Library of Congress.

ISBN: 978-1-4654-3395-4 (Paperback)
ISBN: 978-1-4654-3394-7 (Hardback)

Color reproduction by Alta Image, UK
Printed and bound in China by South China

Discover more at
www.dk.com

Contents

DK READERS

BEGINNING TO READ 1

ANGRY BIRDS™ TRANSFORMERS

DECEPTIHOGS VERSUS AUTOBIRDS

Written by Ruth Amos

Robot rascals

Snort hello to the Deceptihogs.
They are a gang of very
bad pig robots.
They just love to create chaos!

Energon
Starscream
Pig

Dark
Megatron
Pig

The wicked porkers hunt robotic eggs, called Egg-bots. They want to find them before their Autobird enemies get them.

Soundwave Pig

Galvatron Pig

Lockdown Pig

Autobird Heroes

The Autobirds are a flock of fearless bird robots.

The Deceptihogs don't like these bird warriors.

Bumblebee Bird

Optimus Prime Bird

They often mess up the silly hogs' plans!

The Autobirds will do anything to stop the Deceptihogs from stealing the Egg-bots.

Heatwave the Fire-Bot Bird

Grey Slam Grimlock Bird

From pigs... to robots!

The Deceptihogs and
Autobirds were once just
pigs and birds.

One day, the EggSpark fell
on their home, Piggy Island.

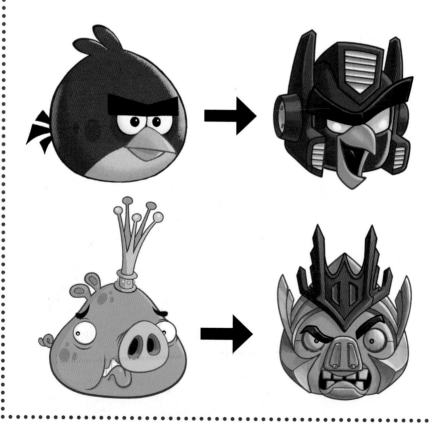

This mysterious source of energy turned all the pigs, birds, and eggs into robots!

EggSpark

Dark Megatron Pig

Make way! Leader of the
Deceptihogs squeezing through!

Dark Megatron Pig
is a little wobbly on
his new robotic legs.
His crown shows
he is top hog, though.

Blaster gun

Megatron believes he
is a champion fighter.
He is not!
He cries like a baby
when he loses, too!

Crown

faceplate

Metallic
faceplate

Awesome tank

Look! Megatron can change into a powerful armored tank.

Bulging eyes

Tank cyberform

This is called his cyberform.

Megatron rumbles around
on huge rolling tracks.
He wants to eat all the Egg-bots
and will blast anyone in his way!

Blaster
cannon

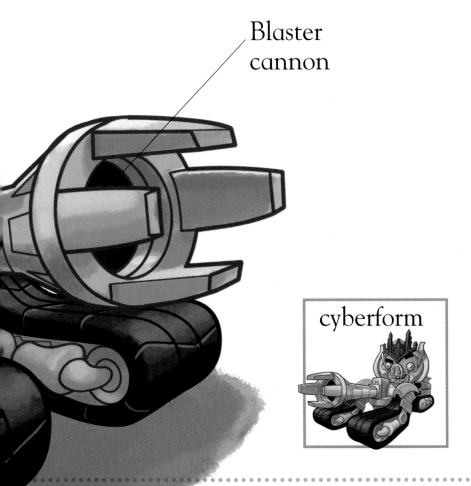

cyberform

Lockdown Pig

Grumpy Lockdown Pig is feared by even the toughest Autobirds and Deceptihogs.

Strong
metal body

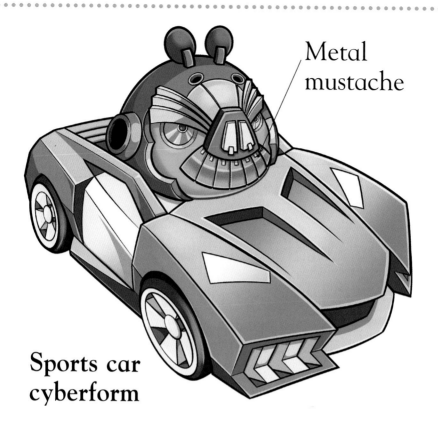

Metal
mustache

**Sports car
cyberform**

Lockdown Pig thinks he
can build anything, but sadly
he is not that smart.
His constructions usually fall
apart in a nano-klik!
On the bright side, he does
turn into a flashy sports car!

Galvatron Pig

Galvatron is mad, bad, and answers to nobody.

This brute is the most powerful Deceptihog. Just don't tell the others!

Galvatron barks out crazy orders to the Deceptihogs. Any hog who does not obey will be blasted into micro-crumbs!

Flatbed truck cyberform

Huge blaster gun

Energon Starscream Pig

Boastful Energon Starscream Pig thinks he has the best combat ideas ever. He snorts at the other Deceptihogs' battle plans.

Plane cyberform

Missile

Upright audioreceptor

Are your audioreceptors
picking something up?
It is Starscream as he flies
to battle in his
noisy jet plane.

audioreceptors

Piggy ambush

Starscream scans Piggy Island and spots an Autobird. The sly pork-bot dive-bombs chunky Heatwave the Fire-Bot Bird.

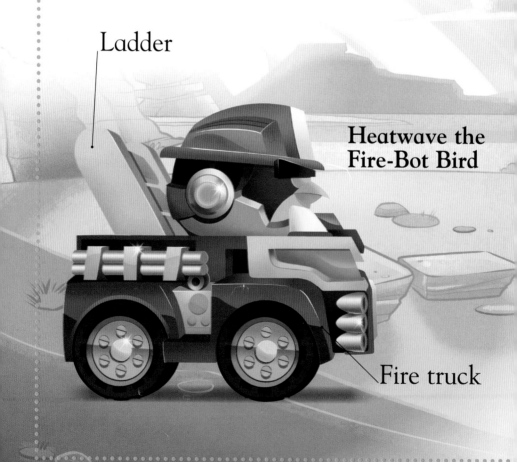

Ladder

Heatwave the Fire-Bot Bird

Fire truck

At the last astrosecond,
Heatwave hears the hog
swooping down.
He extends his ladder
and knocks the wicked
pig far away!

Soundwave Pig

Megatron thinks Soundwave Pig is his most-trusted soldier. Soundwave knows this because he listens in on Megatron with his super-sensitive audioreceptors!

Twirly mustache

Truck cyberform

Sound recorder

They are perfect for spying on
friends and enemies alike.

Smash attack

Evil Soundwave Pig is planning to smash Bumblebee Bird's car into tiny pieces. Oh no! The sneaky swine has a secret weapon.

Soundwave blasts out special sound waves to scramble poor Bumblebee's senses. Luckily, Bumblebee zooms away before the waves damage him!

Bumblebee Bird

sound wave

Clash of the robots

The pig and bird robot armies face each other in a great battle. Cogs, bolts, and chunks of metal fly across the desert!

The Autobirds' strength
and brilliant battle tactics are
too much for the silly swine…
But one thing is certain:
The Deceptihogs will be back!

Quiz

1. What do the Deceptihogs hunt?

2. Which member of the Autobirds is this?

3. Where do the Deceptihogs live?

4. What is this mysterious source of energy called?

5. Who is the leader of the Deceptihogs?

6. Which Deceptihog changes into a sports car?

7. Which member of the Deceptihogs is this?

8. Which Deceptihog turns into a plane?

9. What does Heatwave the Fire-Bot Bird have on his truck that he can use as a weapon?

10. Who listens in on Dark Megatron Pig?

1. Egg-bots, 2. Bumblebee Bird, 3. Piggy Island, 4. The EggSpark, 5. Dark Megatron Pig, 6. Lockdown Pig, 7. Galvatron Pig, 8. Energon Starscream Pig, 9. A ladder, 10. Soundwave Pig

Glossary

EggSpark
A mysterious source of power.

faceplate
A covering that protects a robot's face.

cyberform
A robot's vehicle form.

audioreceptors
A robot's ears.

sound wave
A wave that is formed when a sound is made.

Index

Here are some other DK Readers you might enjoy.

Level 1

Angry Birds™ *Star Wars*® II: Darth Swindle's Secrets
Wicked Darth Swindle has many secrets!
Learn all about this sly swine and his pesky pals.

The LEGO® Movie: Calling All Master Builders!
Who are the Master Builders? Do they have what
it takes to stop Lord Business's evil plans?

***Star Wars*® Are Ewoks Scared of Stormtroopers?**
Meet the bravest heroes in the *Star Wars* galaxy,
who defeat evil villains against all odds.

Level 2

Angry Birds™ Transformers: Robot Birds in Disguise
Piggy Island is under attack! Meet the brave Autobirds.
Can they save their home before it's too late?

Angry Birds™ *Star Wars*®: Lard Vader's Villains
Meet Lard Vader and the Empire Pigs
as they try to take control of the galaxy.

The LEGO® Movie: Awesome Adventures
Meet Emmet and join him on his extraordinary
quest to save the universe!